ANTHOLOGY

Clarinet & PIANO

Christmas duets

Recording cast on CD:

Clarinet: ANDREA PUFFI
Piano: SABRINA DENTE

Recorded by Fabio Bertin @ Studio ecologico PONGO – Locate Varesino

the best on-line resource for music
www.carisch.com
click your music everywhere!

Questo album © 2011 da
CARISCH S.p.A.
Via Canova, 55 - 20020 Lainate (MI)
Tutti i diritti riservati. Ogni riproduzione e/o utilizzazione non autorizzata
verrà perseguita a norma delle leggi civili e penali vigenti. All rights reserved.

ANTHOLOGY

Clarinet & PIANO

JAZZ/SWING DUETS

arrangements with piano accompaniment by Andrea Cappellari

Blue moon
Chattanooga choo choo
Fly me to the moon
Good news
Singin' in the rain
Somebody is knocking at your door
Summertime (from Porgy and Bess®)
Swing low, sweet chariot
The Pink Panther
When the Saints go marching in

BLUE MOON

Words by **Lorenz Hart** *- Music by* **Richard Rodgers**

Start:

Track **1•11**

Arrangement and adaptation for Clarinet and Piano by ***Andrea Cappellari***

CHATTANOOGA CHOO CHOO

Words by **M.Gordon** - *Music by* **H.Warren**

Start: C

Track **2•12**

Arrangement and adaptation for Clarinet and Piano by ***Andrea Cappellari***

Moderato

4 mf

8

13

17 2

23 mf 2

28 4

35 4 4

45 4 f

52 (5)

57 2 mf

FLY ME TO THE MOON

Words and Music by ***B. Howard***

Start: C

Track **3•13**

Arrangement and adaptation for Clarinet and Piano by ***Andrea Cappellari***

Allegro moderato

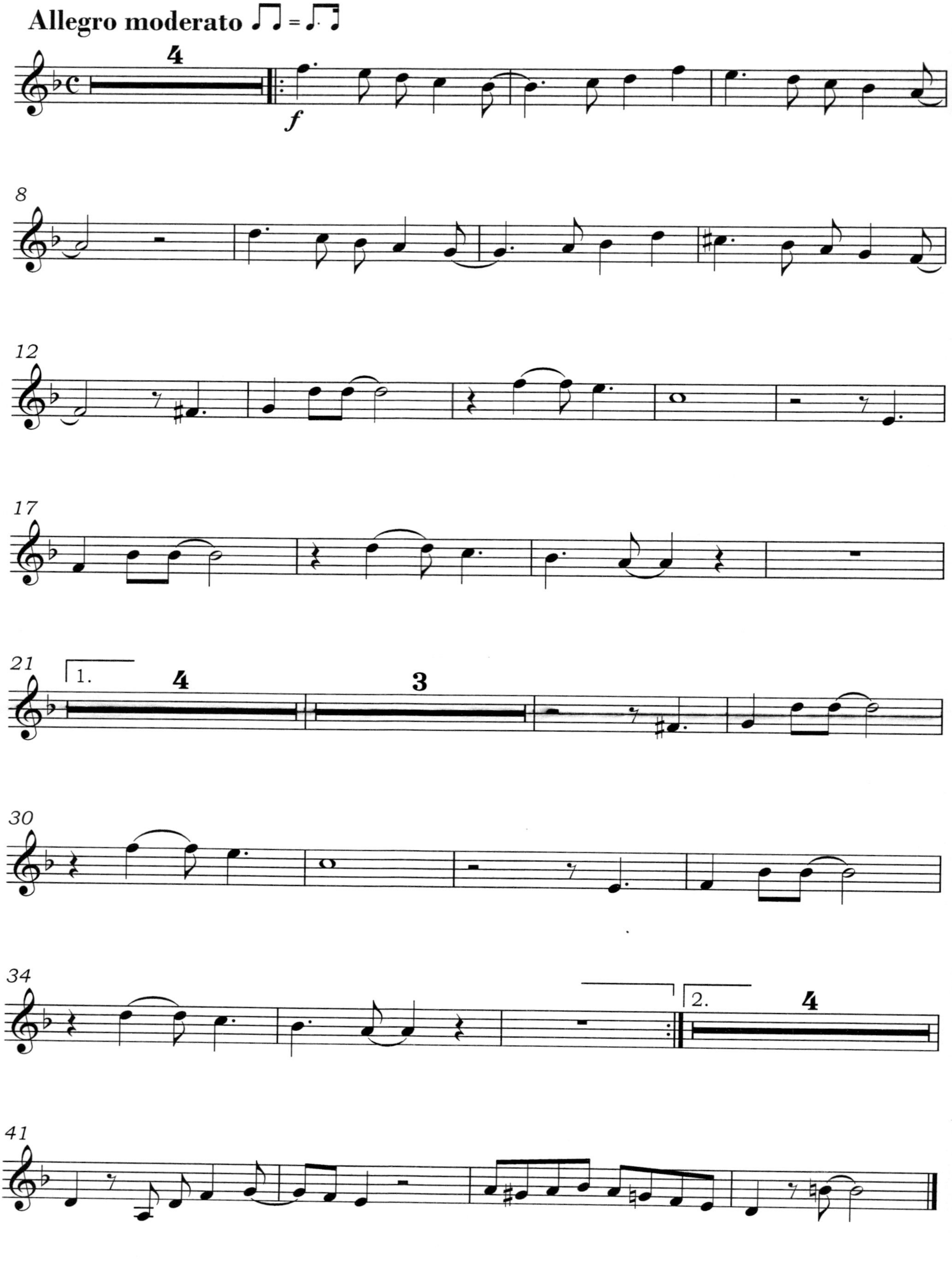

4

f

8

12

17

21

1.

4

3

30

34

2.

4

41

GOOD NEWS

Traditional

Start: 

Arrangement and adaptation for Clarinet and Piano by ***Andrea Cappellari***

Moderato

SINGIN' IN THE RAIN

Words by **Arthur Freed** - *Music by* **Nacio Herb Brown**

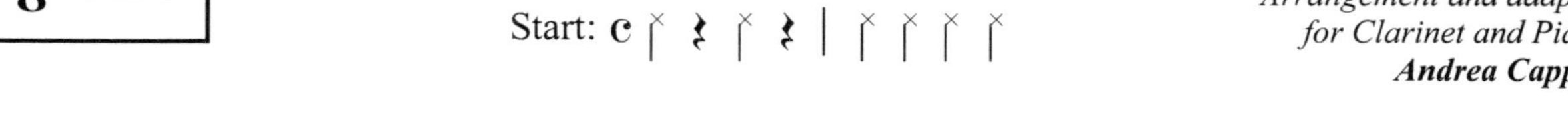

Track **5•15**

Arrangement and adaptation for Clarinet and Piano by **Andrea Cappellari**

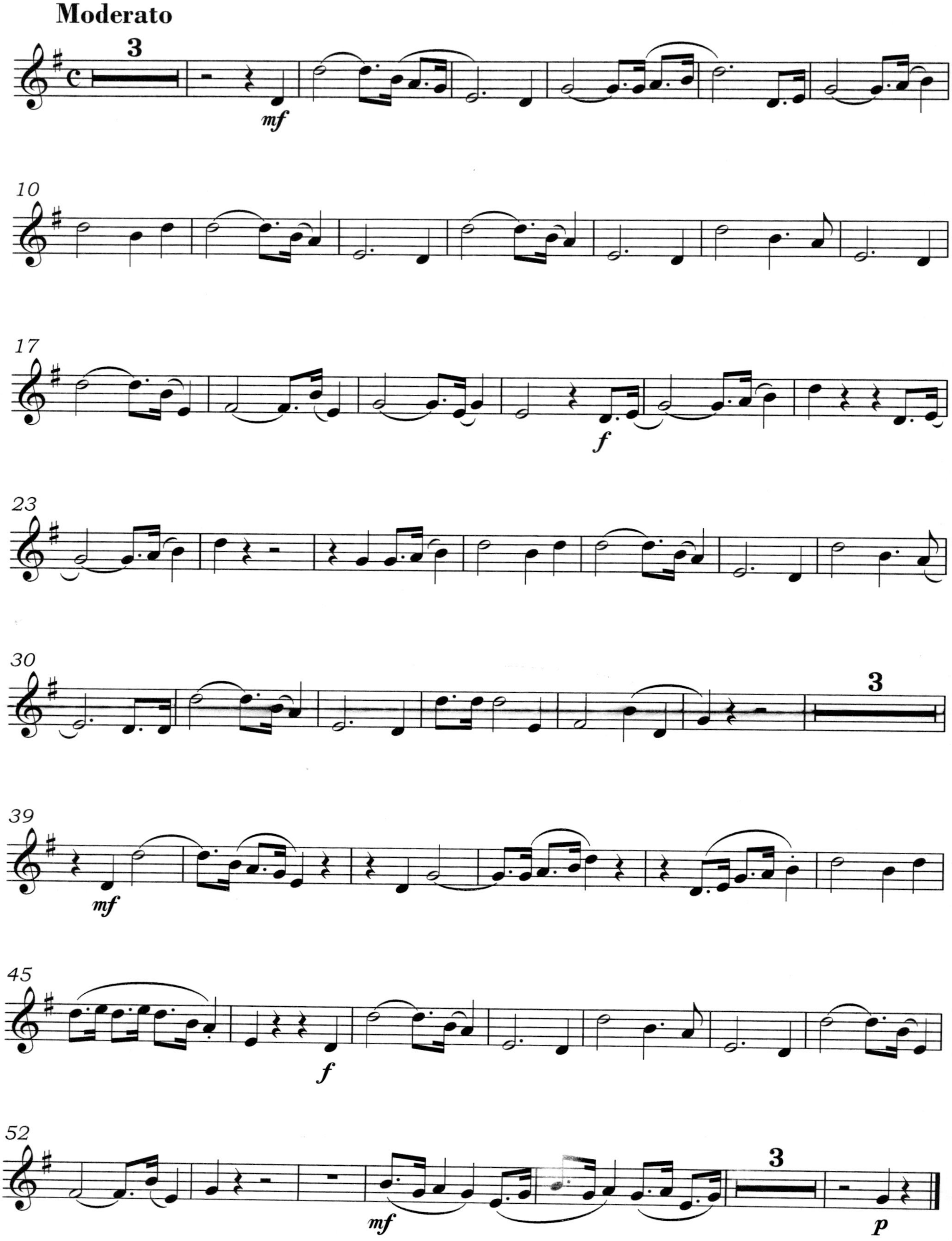

Moderato

3

mf

10

17

f

23

30

3

39

mf

45

f

52

mf

3

p

SOMEBODY IS KNOCKING AT YOUR DOOR

Traditional

Start: 

Track **6•16**

Arrangement and adaptation for Clarinet and Piano by ***Andrea Cappellari***

Andante

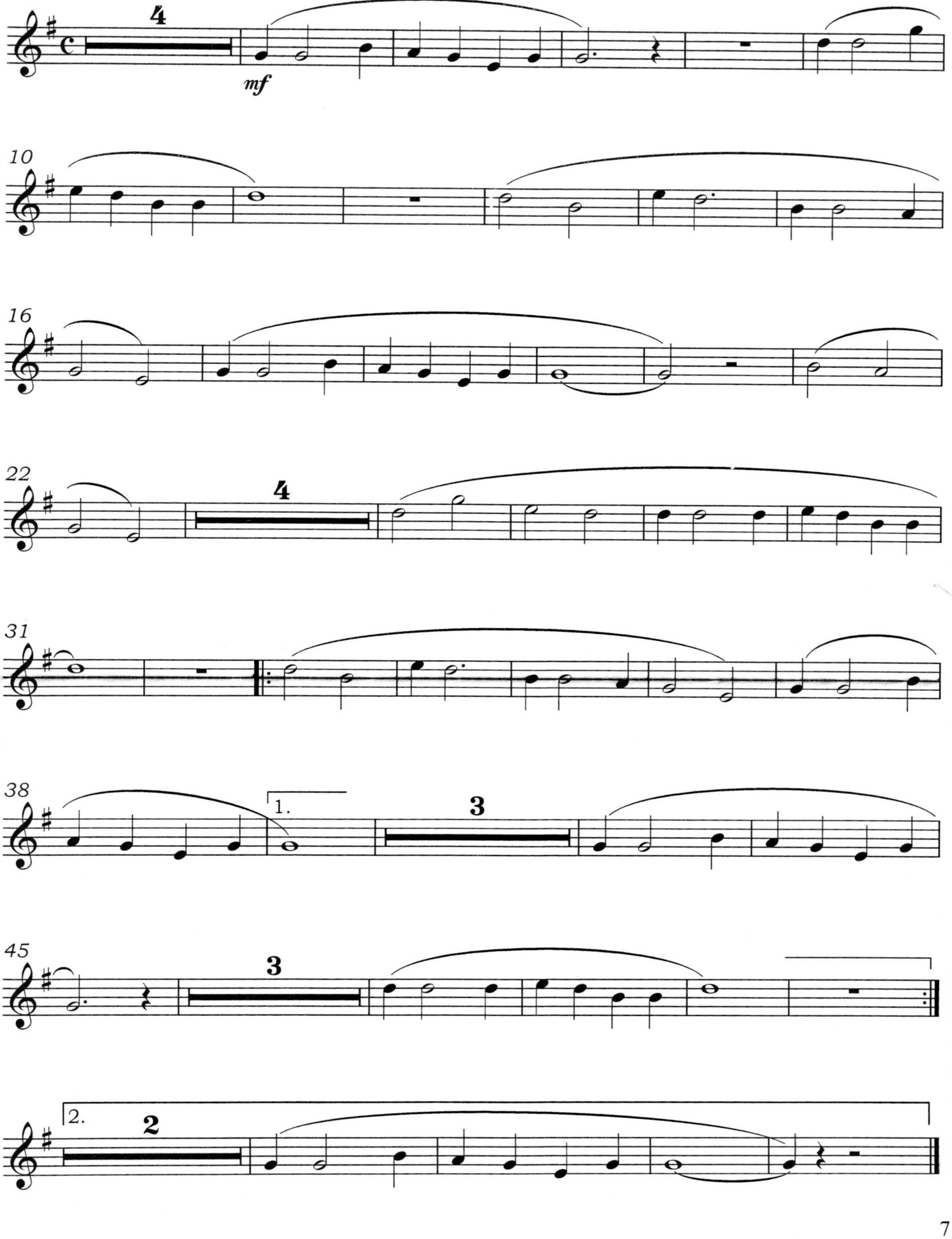

Track
7·17

SUMMERTIME

from "Porgy And Bess®"

Words and Music by ***George Gershwin, Dubose Heyward, Dorothy Heyward, Ira Gershwin***

Arrangement and adaptation for Clarinet and Piano by ***Andrea Cappellari***

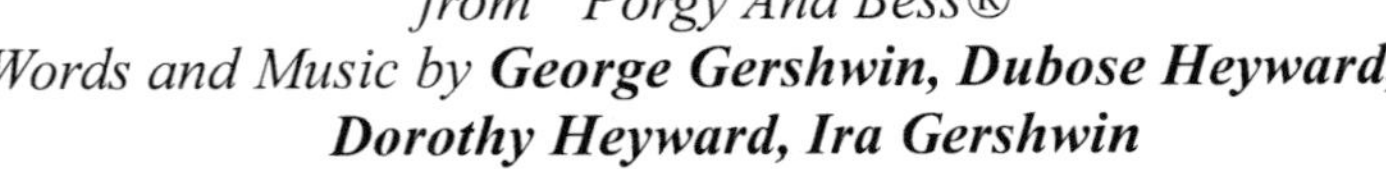

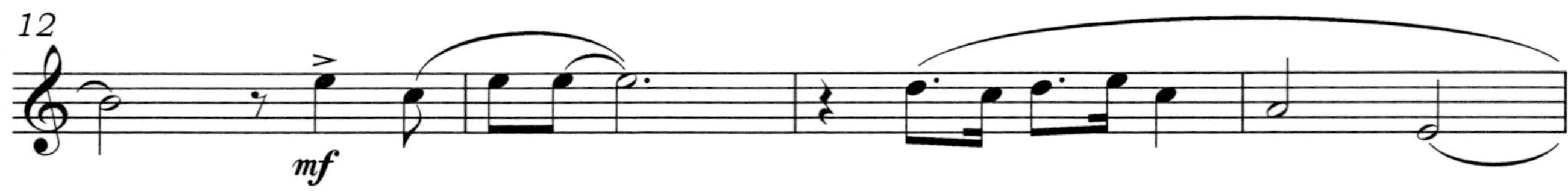

SWING LOW SWEET CHARIOT

Traditional

Start:

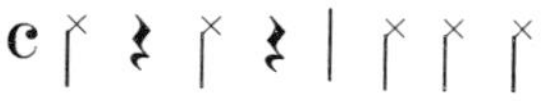

Arrangement and adaptation for Clarinet and Piano by ***Andrea Cappellari***

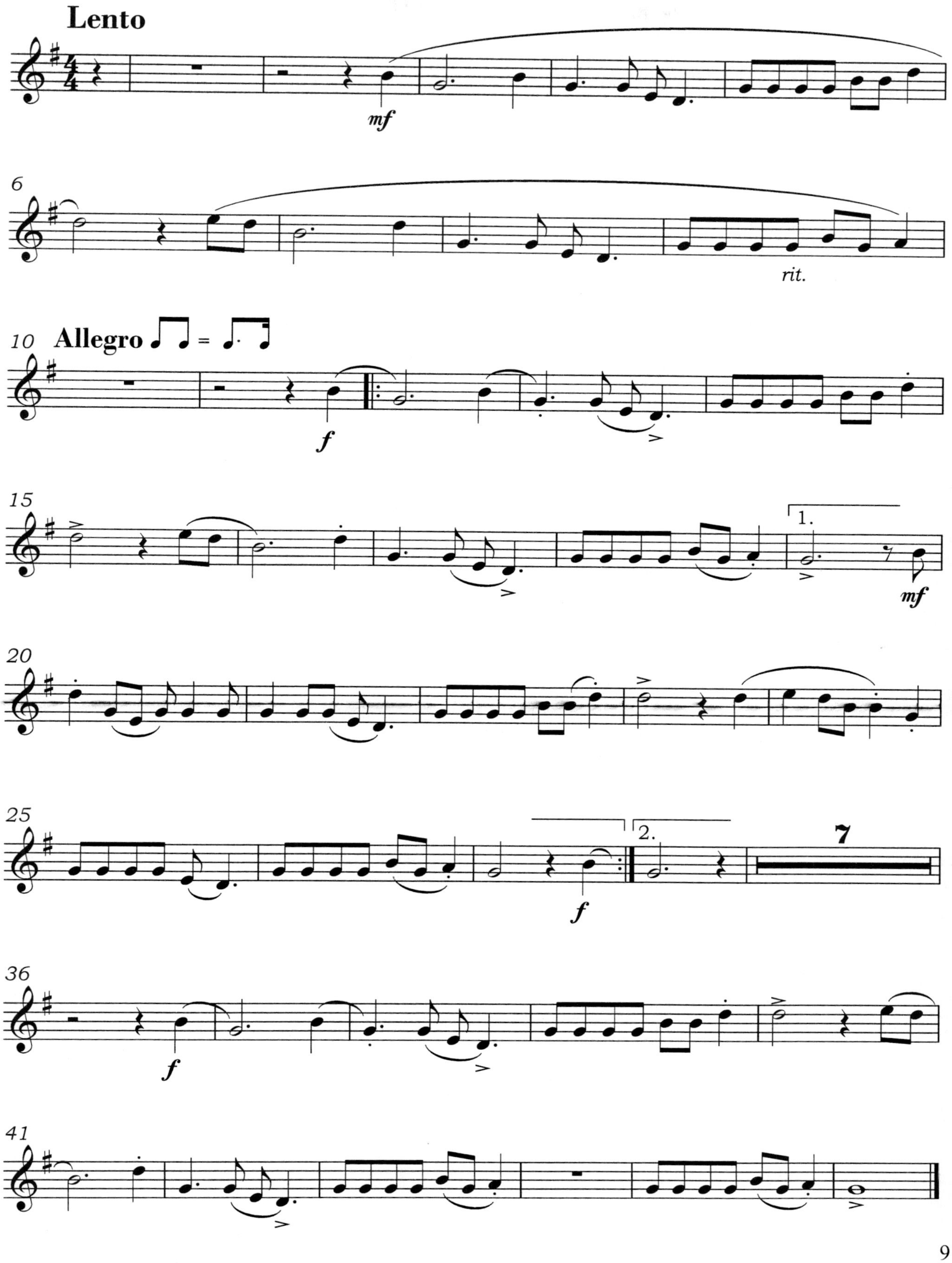

Lento

mf

6

rit.

10 **Allegro**

f

15

1.

mf

20

25

2.

7

f

36

f

41

THE PINK PANTHER

Music by **Henry Mancini**

Start:

Track **9•19**

Arrangement and adaptation for Clarinet and Piano by ***Andrea Cappellari***

Moderato

2 3 *mf*

9 3 3

13

17 3 3 *f*

21 1. 3 *mf*

26

30 (5) 3 3 3

34

2. 3 3

❉ easy version

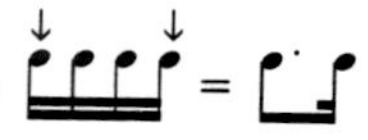

WHEN THE SAINTS GO MARCHING IN

Traditional

Start: **c**

Track **10•20**

Arrangement and adaptation for Clarinet and Piano by ***Andrea Cappellari***

Allegro

7

mf

12

f

17

22

1.

mf

27

32

3

mf

39

f

2.

Clarinet Fingering Chart

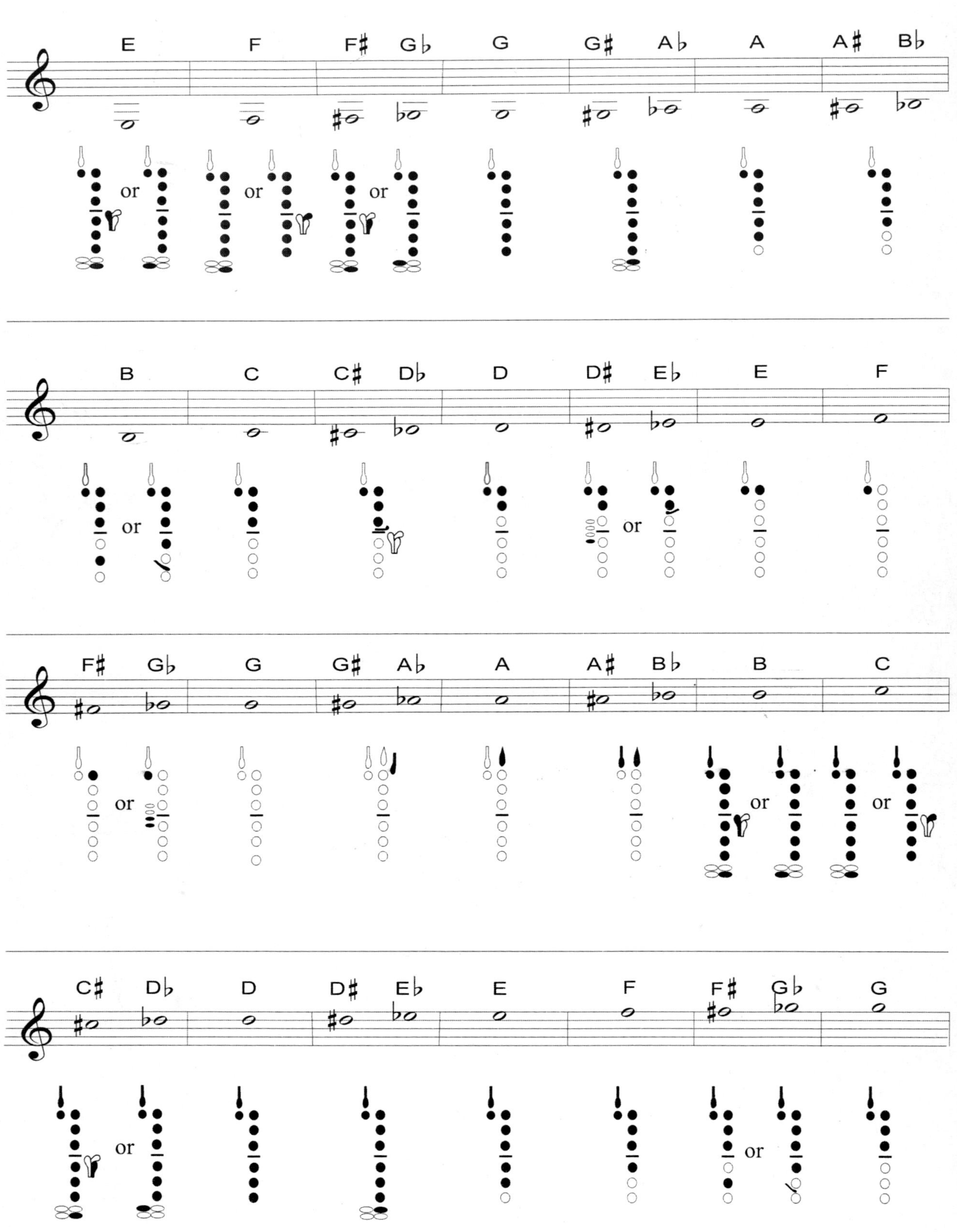

ANTHOLOGY

Clarinet & PIANO

Christmas duets

pag. 2	Adeste Fideles
pag. 3	Deck The Halls
pag. 4	God Rest You Merry Gentlemen
pag. 5	Hark! The Herald Angels Sing
pag. 6	Il Est Né Le Divin Enfant
pag. 7	Jingle Bells
pag. 8	Joy To The World
pag. 9	O Christmas Tree (O Tannenbaum)
pag. 10	The First Nowell
pag. 11	We Wish You A Merry Christmas

ADESTE FIDELES

Words Melody by ***J. F. Wade*** *(1711-1786)*

Start: C

Track **1•11**

Arrangement and adaptation for Clarinet and Piano by ***Andrea Cappellari***

Moderato

3

mf

9

14

p

19

mf

f

23

8

f

36

p

mf

41

f

rit.

DECK THE HALLS

Traditional

Start: 2/4

Track 2•12

Arrangement and adaptation for Clarinet and Piano by ***Andrea Cappellari***

Vivace

8

mf

15

23

p

31

mf

39

4

mf

49

4

58

65

73

2

p

mf

GOD REST YOU MERRY GENTLEMEN

Traditional

Start: ¢

Arrangement and adaptation for Clarinet and Piano by **Andrea Cappellari**

Moderato

7

mf

13

cresc.

18

f

dim.

23

cresc.

29

3

3

7

44

cresc.

50

55

3

f

dim.

63

cresc.

HARK! THE HERALD ANGELS SING

Melody by F. Mendelssohn (1809-1847)

Start: C

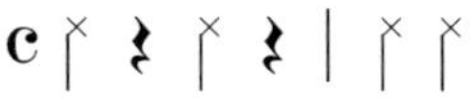

Arrangement and adaptation for Clarinet and Piano by ***Andrea Cappellari***

Allegro moderato

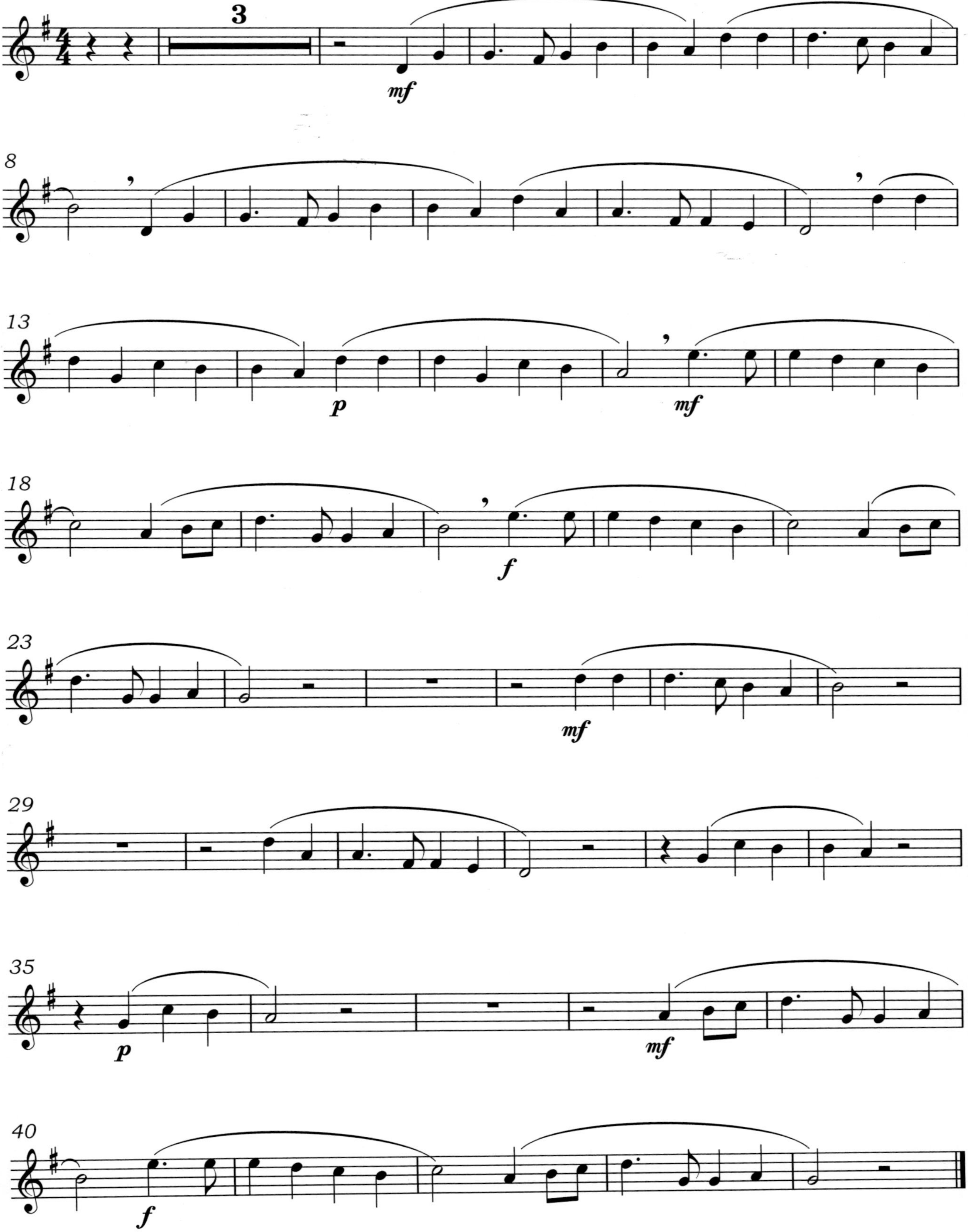

3

mf

8

13

p

mf

18

f

23

mf

29

35

p

mf

40

f

IL EST NÉ LE DIVIN ENFANT

Traditional

Start: ¢

Track **5•15**

Arrangement and adaptation for Clarinet and Piano by ***Andrea Cappellari***

JINGLE BELLS

Words and Melody by ***J.Pierpont (1822-1893)***

Start: 2/4

Track 6•16

Arrangement and adaptation for Clarinet and Piano by ***Andrea Cappellari***

Vivace

4

mf

10

16

21

f

27

33

1

mf

39

46

53

2

JOY TO THE WORLD

Words by ***I.Watts*** *- Music by* ***L.Mason*** *- based on* ***HANDEL***

Start:

Track **7•17**

Arrangement and adaptation for Clarinet and Piano by ***Andrea Cappellari***

Allegretto

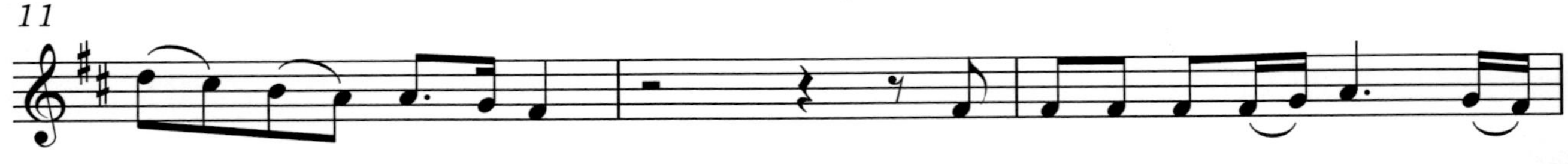

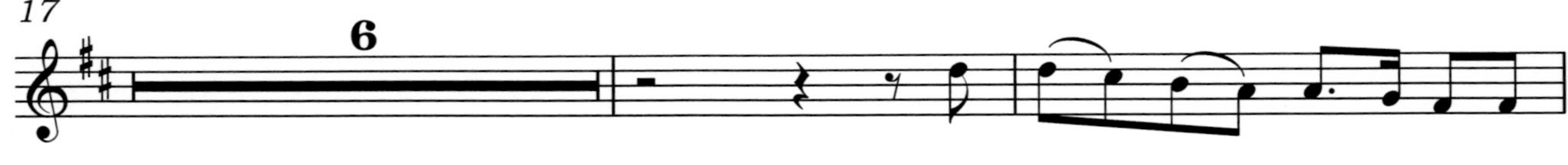

O CHRISTMAS TREE (O Tannenbaum)

Traditional

Start: 3/4

Track 8•18

Arrangement and adaptation for Clarinet and Piano by **Andrea Cappellari**

Moderato

THE FIRST NOWELL

Traditional

Start: 3/4

Arrangement and adaptation for Clarinet and Piano by ***Andrea Cappellari***

Moderato

3

mf

9

17

3

25

31

3

40

47

p

WE WISH YOU A MERRY CHRISTMAS

Traditional

Start: 3/4

Track **10•20**

Arrangement and adaptation for Clarinet and Piano by ***Andrea Cappellari***

Allegro

7

mf

13

20

27

33

7

46

53

59

Clarinet Fingering Chart

pag. 4 Adeste Fideles
pag. 6 Deck The Halls
pag. 8 God Rest You Merry Gentlemen
pag. 10 Hark! The Herald Angels Sing
pag. 12 Il Est Né Le Divin Enfant
pag. 14 Jingle Bells
pag. 16 Joy To The World
pag. 18 O Christmas Tree (O Tannenbaum)
pag. 20 The First Nowell
pag. 22 We Wish You A Merry Christmas

ADESTE FIDELES

Words Melody by ***J. F. Wade*** *(1711-1786)*

Start: C

Track **1•11**

Arrangement and adaptation for Clarinet and Piano by ***Andrea Cappellari***

Moderato

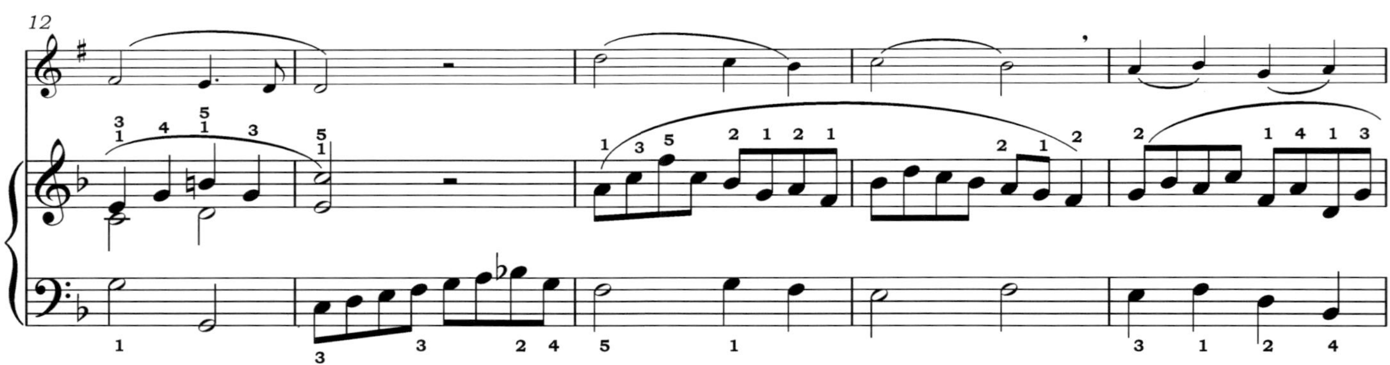

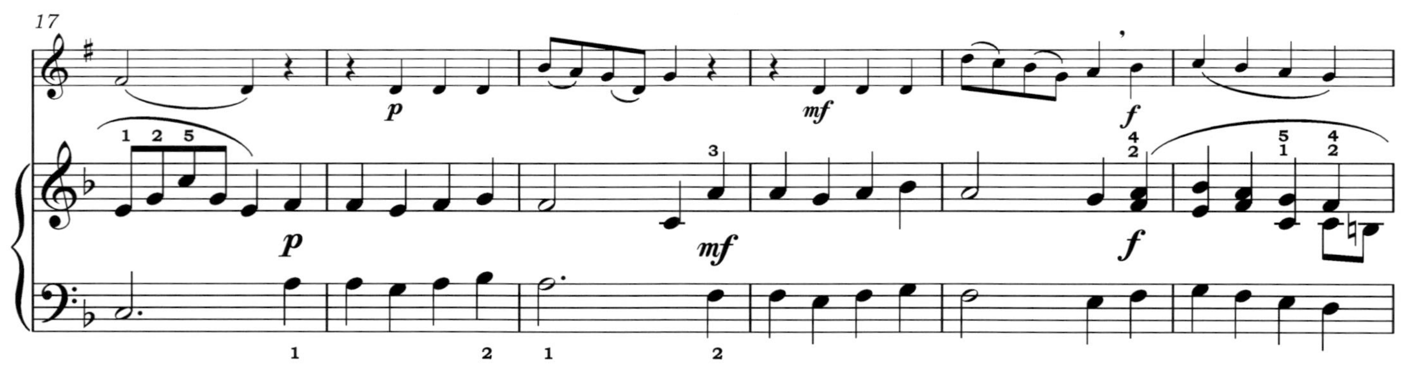

This transcription by © 2011 by CARISCH SpA. - Via Canova, 55 - 20020 Lainate (MI)
All rights reserved. International Copyright secured.

23
dim.
f

29
f
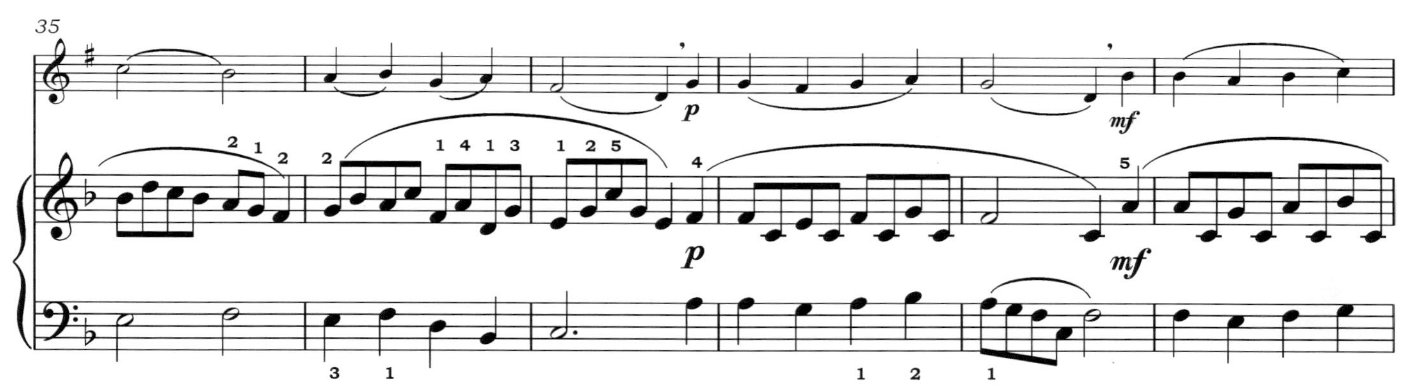
35
p
mf

41
f
rit.

DECK THE HALLS

Traditional

Track 2•12

Arrangement and adaptation for Clarinet and Piano by ***Andrea Cappellari***

This transcription by © 2011 by CARISCH SpA. - Via Canova, 55 - 20020 Lainate (MI)
All rights reserved. International Copyright secured.

41
mf
f
49
57
65
72
p
mf

GOD REST YOU MERRY GENTLEMEN

Traditional

Track 3•13

Arrangement and adaptation for Clarinet and Piano by
Andrea Cappellari

This transcription by © 2011 by CARISCH SpA. - Via Canova, 55 - 20020 Lainate (MI)
All rights reserved. International Copyright secured.

35
cresc.
f
42
cresc.
cresc.
49
56
f
cresc.
f
62
dim.
cresc.
dim.
cresc.

HARK! THE HERALD ANGELS SING

Melody by F. Mendelssohn (1809-1847)

Start:

Track **4•14**

Arrangement and adaptation for Clarinet and Piano by ***Andrea Cappellari***

Allegro moderato

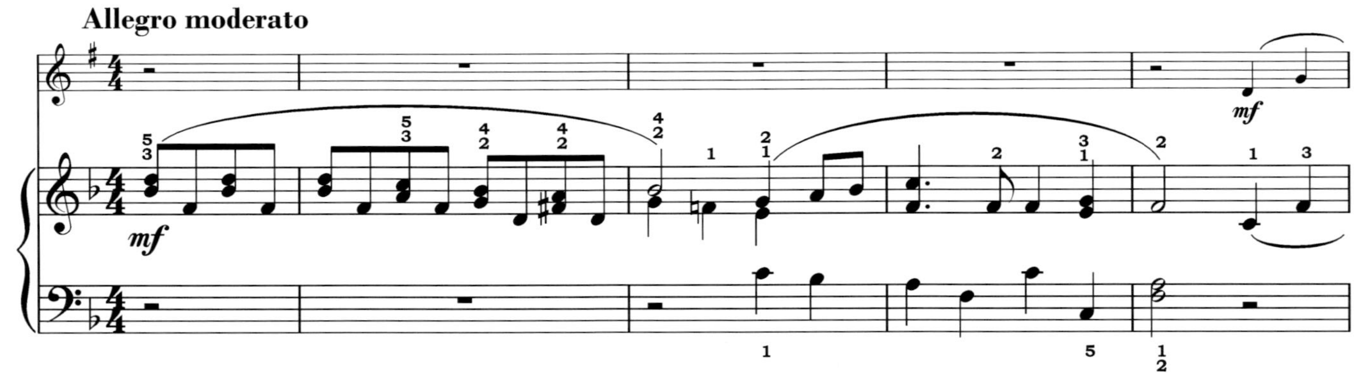

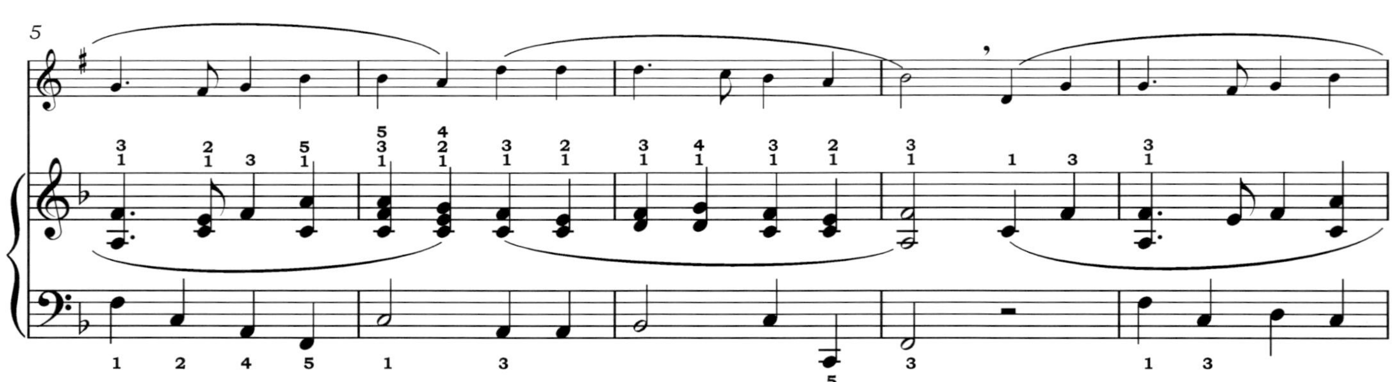

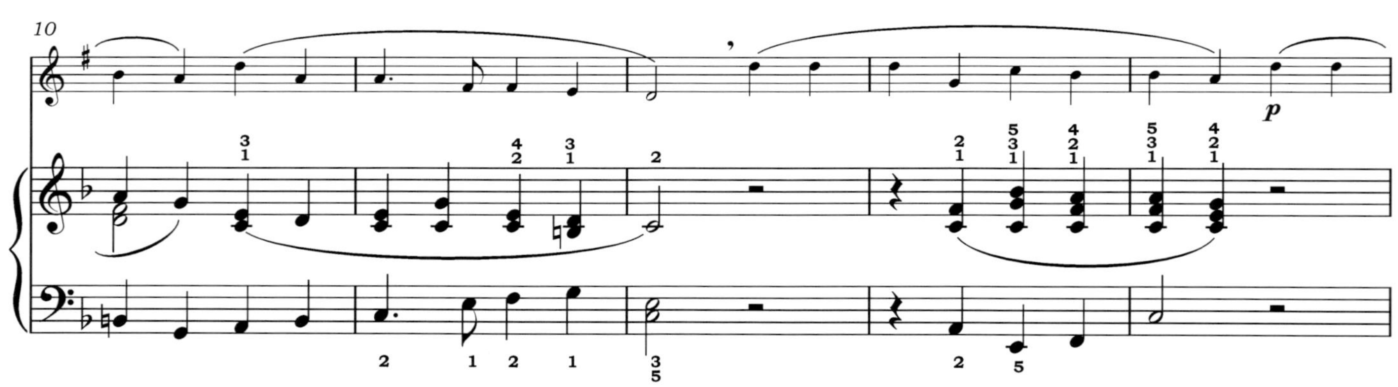

This transcription by © 2011 by CARISCH SpA. - Via Canova, 55 - 20020 Lainate (MI)
All rights reserved. International Copyright secured.

20
f
f
mf
25
mf
30
p
35
p
mf
mf
40
f
f

IL EST NÉ LE DIVIN ENFANT

Traditional

Track **5•15**

Arrangement and adaptation for Clarinet and Piano by ***Andrea Cappellari***

Start: ¢

This transcription by © 2011 by CARISCH SpA. - Via Canova, 55 - 20020 Lainate (MI)
All rights reserved. International Copyright secured.

26
mf
32
38
44
mf
50

JINGLE BELLS

Words and Melody by ***J.Pierpont (1822-1893)***

Track
6•16

Arrangement and adaptation for Clarinet and Piano by ***Andrea Cappellari***

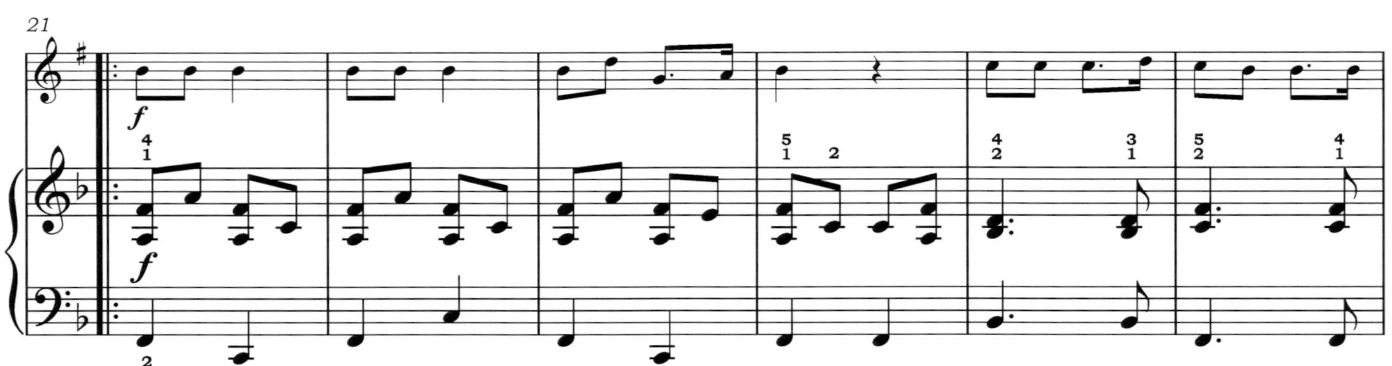

This transcription by © 2011 by CARISCH SpA. - Via Canova, 55 - 20020 Lainate (MI)
All rights reserved. International Copyright secured.

27
33
1
mf
mf
40
f
47
53
2

JOY TO THE WORLD

Words by **I.Watts** - *Music by* **L.Mason** - *based on* **HANDEL**

Track **7•17**

Arrangement and adaptation for Clarinet and Piano by **Andrea Cappellari**

Start:

This transcription by © 2011 by CARISCH SpA. - Via Canova, 55 - 20020 Lainate (MI)
All rights reserved. International Copyright secured.

16
f

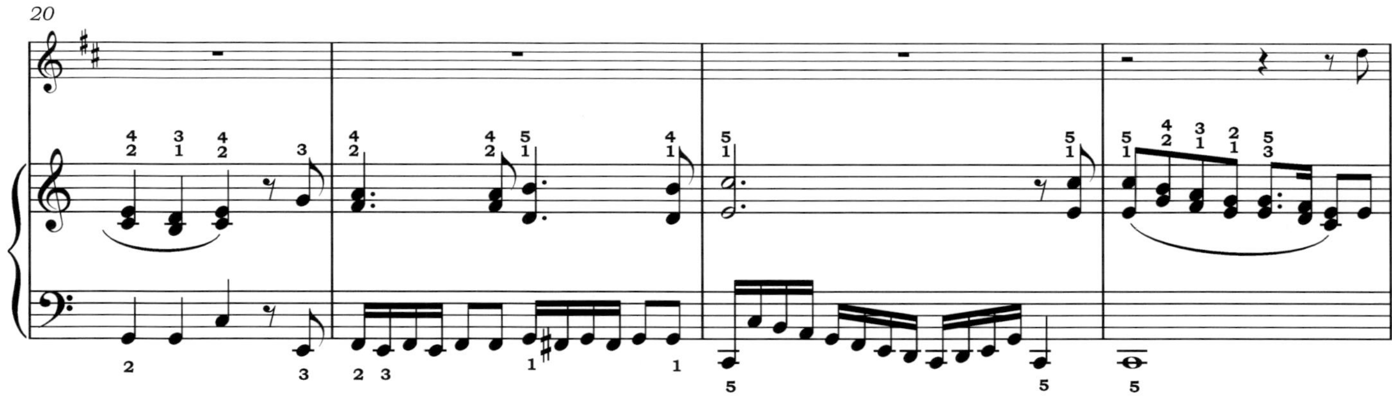
20

24

28
rit.
rit.

O CHRISTMAS TREE (O Tannenbaum)

Traditional

Track **8 • 18**

Arrangement and adaptation for Clarinet and Piano by ***Andrea Cappellari***

Start: 3/4

Moderato

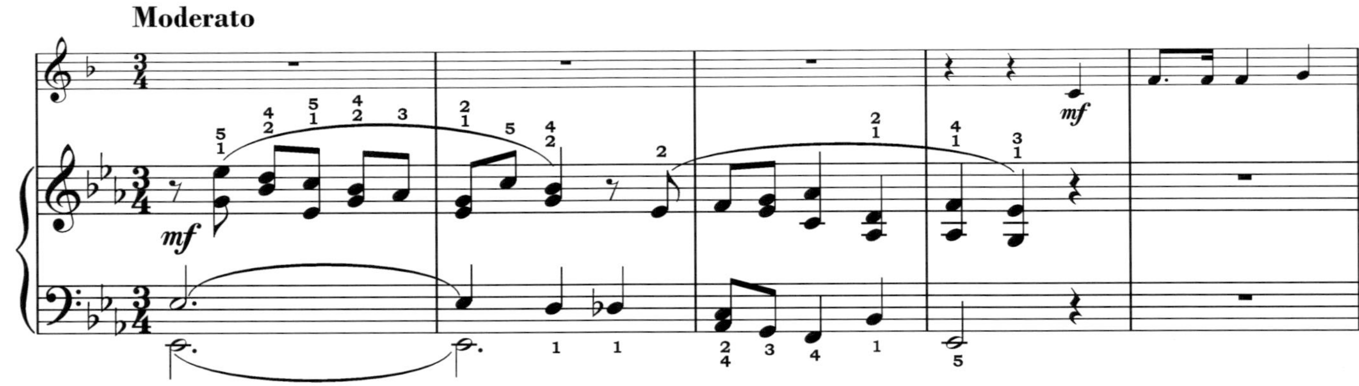

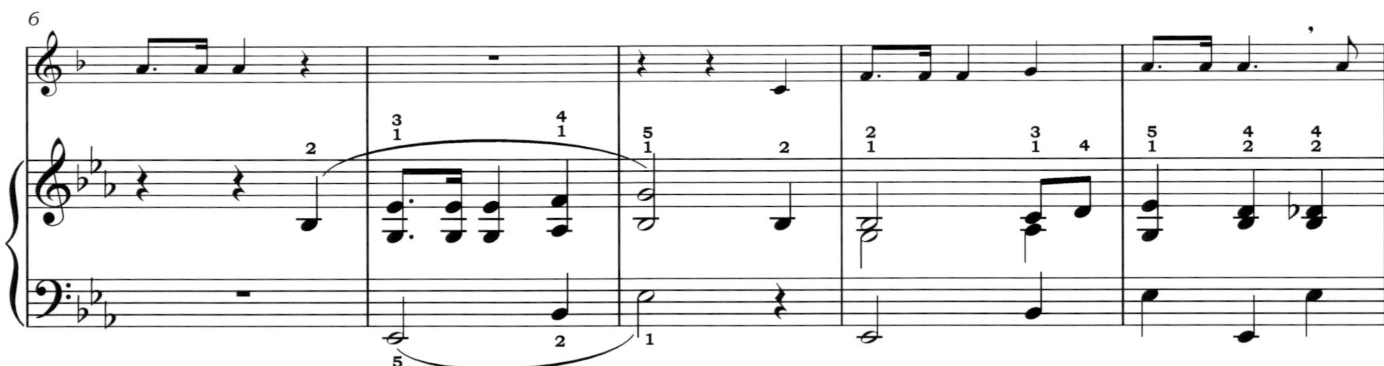

This transcription by © 2011 by CARISCH SpA. - Via Canova, 55 - 20020 Lainate (MI)
All rights reserved. International Copyright secured.

20
25
29
34
39

THE FIRST NOWELL

Traditional

Start: 3/4

Track 9•19

Arrangement and adaptation for Clarinet and Piano by ***Andrea Cappellari***

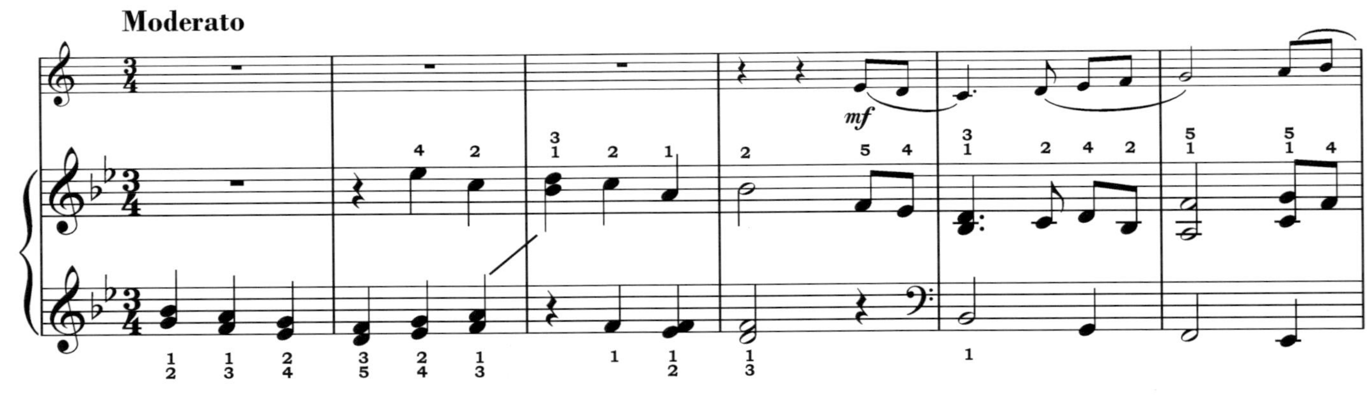

This transcription by © 2011 by CARISCH SpA. - Via Canova, 55 - 20020 Lainate (MI)
All rights reserved. International Copyright secured.

24
p
cresc.
dim.
30
cresc.
35
41
p
cresc.
47
dim.
p
p

WE WISH YOU A MERRY CHRISTMAS

Traditional

Track 10•20

Arrangement and adaptation for Clarinet and Piano by
Andrea Cappellari

Start: 3/4

This transcription by © 2011 by CARISCH SpA. - Via Canova, 55 - 20020 Lainate (MI)
All rights reserved. International Copyright secured.

33
40
47
53
59